PREPARE THE WAY

SERMON BOOK

PREPARE THE WAY
SERMON BOOK

Sermons and Sermonic Studies
for Advent and Christmas

George W. Bornemann

Publishing House
St. Louis

Copyright © 1988 Concordia Publishing House
3558 S. Jefferson Avenue, St. Louis, MO 63118-3968
Manufactured in the United States of America

1   2   3   4   5   6   7   8   9   10   VP   97   96   95   94   93   92   91   90   89   88

Contents

Preface and Suggestions 7

Advent 1 9
Prepare the Way: Get Ready and Prepare
Mark 1:1—4

Advent 2 15
Prepare the Way: With Prophets of God
Luke 1:55, 70

Advent 3 21
Prepare the Way: By Repentance
Matthew 3:2; Mark 1:14—15

Advent 4 27
Prepare the Way: We Believe and Trust
Luke 1:18, 34

Christmas Eve 31
Prepare the Way: Celebrating Jesus Christ as the Way
Luke 2:10—11; John 14:6

Christmas Day 37
Prepare the Way: Rejoicing in the Way
Luke 2:10—11, 20

New Year's Eve 43
Prepare the Way: Memories of His Mercies
Luke 1:67—75

New Year's Day 49
Prepare the Way: For Our Future
Luke 1:76—79

Epiphany 55
Prepare the Way: For Others
John 1:6—16

Preface and Suggestions

Advent is preparation time for Christmas, as Lent is preparation time for Easter. While Lent is taken more seriously in the church, as it precedes crucifixion and resurrection, deeds which bring home to us personally our Savior's sacrifice for sins, Advent seems mild as it follows the joyful Thanksgiving season and shortly precedes Christmas and New Year, surrounded by commercialism.

Lent attempts to end its pre-Lenten season with a bash of Mardi Gras. There is no such ending for Thanksgiving joy prior to Advent, and there is no need to manufacture one.

For many Advent is a time for choral concerts and children's programs. (What else will bring people out midweek in winter?) It may become advantageous to make it an emphasis on the end of the world, the judgment of God, hopelessness around us, with nothing left but Christmas joy.

While Lent can be personal with repentance, forgiveness, and salvation for us, perhaps Advent might shift too.—But wait!

The message of Christmas is there with its tidings of great joy, and it has its shadows of killing babes. It has a worldly touch of census and taxes and emphasis on superpowers. With New Year there are plenty of themes on accountability and on new chances.

(It is suggested that these sermon themes be used at special— not Sunday—services and that, where possible, references be included in the sermon to the family's daily devotional booklet in this series.)

Advent 1

Prepare the Way

Get Ready and Prepare

Mark 1:1–4

Notes

Prepare the way for the coming of God - whether for judgment or salvation. With the world going its own way it may be soon time to shift to a new gear and emphasize the judgment. But the Gospel, not the scary tactics of Armageddon or earth's wars and quaking are in order. In either case repentance is needed, and the call of Amos (4:12) is there: "Therefore thus I will do to you, O Israel; because I will do this to you, prepare to meet your God, O Israel."

Israel spent much time in preparing for its celebration of a Passover, with remembrance of deliverance from slavery. Noah spent time in preparing an ark for God's judgment. To celebrate our deliverance from a judgment which we deserve, there is time and place to prepare.

"Prepare the way" is the cry of prophets Isaiah and Malachi, answered by John the Baptist as he prepared the way for the coming Christ.

This Advent we prepare, studying the need, the thrust of repentance, the assurances of promised salvation, the revelation in Jesus Christ, the gratitude for past mercies, the prayer for future direction, and the need of sharing Him who is the Way with those who know Him not.

Blessings as you prepare the way this Advent!

The Sermon

All four evangelists say the same about John the forerunner, but Mark places him at the Gospel's opening. He writes (Mark 1:1–4): "The beginning of the Gospel of Jesus Christ, the Son of God. As it is written in Isaiah the prophet, 'Behold, I send my messenger before thy face, who shall prepare thy way; the voice of one crying in the wilderness: Prepare the way of the Lord, make his paths straight—' John the Baptizer appeared in the wilderness, preaching a baptism of repentance for the forgiveness of sins." This is where the Gospel begins, for it is good news being realized that the forerunner of the Savior appears and makes the heraldic announcement, "Prepare the way." Clear the road, remove all obstacles. Whatever you are doing, get ready for the Lord.

The voice of John, as said the prophet, is from the wilderness. Yet when John the Baptist speaks, he is more than a voice in the wilderness crying, "Prepare the way."

When people asked John a simple question, "What shall we do?" he told them (Luke 3) to "bear fruits that befit repentance," such as sharing food and clothing, refraining from cheating in the taxing process and from using force and violence, because these actions must meet judgment, and the Judge is ready with flame to burn all that is chaff, not wheat. The evil is to be harvested and burnt.

"Prepare the way," said the prophets Isaiah and Malachi. They teach us more about how and why to prepare the way. To understand any Scripture passage, it is best to ask Scripture itself for the interpretation.

Isaiah wrote a long book of 66 chapters. Chapters 40 to 66 are full of hope and promise, a vision which God lays out because of His grace and goodness. The section is almost like another gospel, for it talks of salvation and mercy, grace and love. The Ethiopian eunuch read that section while traveling along the way from Jerusalem to Egypt, down the Gaza strip. When Philip asked him, "Do you understand what you are reading?" he answered, "How can I, unless someone guides me?" (Acts 8:30–31). Philip explained that Isaiah was talking about the good news that comes to us in Jesus. And that's the key to Isaiah. Chapters 40 to 66 are filled with songs and oracles of hope and strength, dealing especially with news of a Messiah, a Suffering Servant of God, by whom salvation comes. Look at the Christ in the crib and on the cross, and then Isaiah explains itself.

Look at what went immediately before these oracles. Isaiah 39 recounts a meeting of King Hezekiah with the representatives of Babylon, a superpower. Trying to appease this hostile force, the king showed them all his treasures, gems, gold, armament. Nothing was hidden. Isaiah the prophet asked him about the visit, and hearing the king's report he told him of his foolish mistake, because Babylon was ready to absorb Palestine. God allows it to happen, as He does so often in our own lives, because of sins unrepented. Hezekiah's children, he says, will not be able to stand. Strangely King Hezekiah felt good, for he thought time was on his side, trouble would not touch him. Peace and security would be sure in his days.

Against that background Isaiah looks into the future and gives an oracle of a loving Lord who longs to show love, who cares enough to give pardon and bring His people safely home. What a Lord we have, giving punishment yet in its midst planning pardon! Isaiah later writes of a Suffering Servant, wounded for our transgressions and bruised for our iniquities, upon whom comes chastisement for our peace.

Chapter 40 opens as God speaks: "Comfort, comfort my people, says your God. Speak tenderly to Jerusalem, and cry to her that her warfare is ended, that her iniquity is pardoned, that she has received from the Lord's hand double for all her sins." This is the continuing, constant voice of our God, who has compassion and love for all of us, who sees our sin and knows our deserved punishment. God so wants not to condemn the sinner, but that the sinner be pardoned and live. But punishment must come. Discipline for wrongs must be meted out. It is a tough love.

Isaiah says that *three voices* are heard. The first voice says that Israel shall return home to Jerusalem, the enemy will be crushed, and the world will see God vindicate His own. The voice says, "Prepare the way in the wilderness for God, for we are coming home."

The second voice says, "Cry! Speak out." Isaiah asks, "What shall I cry?" The voice says that all things vanish and pass away as grass and wild flowers die, but God's Word abides, His promises are sure.

A third voice cries to Jerusalem, "Get up on Mount Zion. Speak strongly, loudly, clearly, that God comes in might. Be a herald on the mountaintop. Cry out! God will be Lord. He will rule." And the same voice talks about the mighty Lord being a shepherd, leading His flock, gathering His lambs in His arm and embracing them.

And that is what happened! Christ, the Good Shepherd, laid down His life for the sheep and conquered all our enemies—the flesh, the evil world, the power of sin, and our last enemy, death. When Mark begins the good news of Jesus, he properly takes those very words of Isaiah and by the power of the Spirit shows their fulfillment in John the Baptist, for we read: "As it is written in Isaiah . . . 'Behold, I send my messenger [my herald], before [God] . . . the voice of one crying in the wilderness: Prepare the way of the Lord, make His paths straight—'" The Lord comes to rule, to conquer, to overcome. He comes as a shepherd to lead His flock and gather the lambs in His bosom.

That's what Advent is about. We get ready, prepare, to receive Him, for in Him we behold the Destroyer of death, the Subduer of Satan, the Savior from sin, bringing each of us back from our exile into our Father's house, that we may live and remain in His heavenly home forever.

King Hezekiah displayed to his enemies the treasures of his home and country. Tricking the sick and weak king, they took note of everything in preparation for the time when Babylon would devour his land and people. It is something like that which happens to us when "the devil prowls around like a roaring lion, seeking someone to devour" (1 Peter 5:8). The talents and gifts God gave us to do good are used for the evil of this world and our flesh, and because of our foolish and weak ways we are in danger of being taken from our home, our heavenly home. God is concerned. The time of His coming, His advent, is here. "Prepare the way," for God will overcome sin and death and hell by that Child in the manger.

We said there were two prophets whose words, "Prepare the way" were used by and about John the Baptist. The first was Isaiah, the second was Malachi. The Book of Malachi, a short one, is the last book in the Old Testament.

The temple had been destroyed by the enemy which took its treasures. Two exiled patriots, Ezra and Nehemiah, had asked and received permission to return and rebuild the city and temple. Instead of joy and gratitude, the same old sins and even some new ones developed as people neglected offerings and tithes, priests abused sacrifices and mocked at prayer, services were empty of God's Word, and the Law was ignored.

Malachi says the Lord will come to His temple, to the house of the Lord, and will refine it with the refiner's fire used on silver, and cleanse it with strong soap. God says through Malachi: "Behold, I send My messenger to prepare the way before Me, and the Lord whom you seek will suddenly come to His temple ... behold, He is coming.... But who can endure the day of His coming?" He will come for judgment against adultery, lies, cheating, oppression. Malachi closes the book as God says: "Behold, I will send you Elijah the prophet before the great and terrible day of the Lord comes."

John the Baptist, with Jesus' support, says he is the messenger preparing the way for the coming of the Lord. John comes to prepare for Jesus, the Lord, of whom the prophet speaks. It is the Lord Jesus whom John points to as "the Lamb of God, who takes away the sin of the world." Moreover, it is Jesus who has been given judgment by the Father, having His fork in His hand, ready to separate chaff from wheat. About Elijah coming? Jesus told His disciples that Elijah came in John. Once Jesus came to save, but He returns for judgment.

And while we prepare now to celebrate the comfort Isaiah talks about, we see on the horizon—still in our future, for we know not when He will suddenly return—the day and hour when He will separate wheat from chaff, sheep from goats, righteous from unrighteous. We cannot prepare for His first coming without looking forward with joy to His return. The grace, compassion, love, and kindness of the Lord comes with all its "Glory to God in the highest" at Bethlehem, but the return of our Lord to take His very own to Himself also is before us this Advent.

So with one look God prepares the way so we exiles can return; with another look John helps us prepare the way for the Lord as He comes at His return.

Advent 2

Prepare the Way

With Prophets of God

Luke 1:55, 70

Notes

God's Son	Ps. 2:7	Luke 1:32, 35
Woman's seed	Gen. 3:15	Gal. 4:4
Abraham's seed	Gen. 17:7; 22:18	Gal. 3:16
Isaac's seed	Gen. 21:12	Heb. 11:17–19
David's seed	Ps. 132:11; Jer. 23:5	Acts 13:23; Rom. 1:3
Time for coming	Gen. 49:10	Luke 2:1; Gal. 4:4
Virgin birth	Is. 7:14	Matt. 1:22–23
Immanuel	Is. 7:14	Matt. 1:22–23
Bethlehem birth	Micah 5:2	Matt. 2:1; Luke 2:4–6
Kings adore	Ps. 72:10	Matt. 2:1–11
Children slain	Jer. 31:15	Matt. 2:16–18
Called from Egypt	Hos. 11:1	Matt. 2:15
John the Baptist	Is. 40:3; Mal. 3:1	Matt. 3:1, 3; Luke 1:17
Spirit anointed	Ps. 45:7; Is. 11:2; 61:1	Matt 3:16; John 3:34; Acts 10:38
Moses—prophet	Deut. 18:15–18	Acts 3:20–22
Melchizedek—priest	Ps. 110:4	Heb. 5:5–6
Public ministry	Is. 61:1–2	Luke 4:16–21, 43
Galilean ministry	Is. 9:1–2	Matt. 4:12–16, 23
Enters Jerusalem	Zech. 9:9	Matt. 21:1–5
Comes to temple	Hag. 2:7–9; Mal. 3:1	Matt. 21:12; Luke 2:27–32; John 2:13–16
Poverty	Is. 53:2	Mark 6:3; Luke 9:58
Meek	Is. 42:2	Matt. 11:29
Tender	Is. 40:11; 42:3	Matt. 12:15, 20; Heb. 4:15
No guile	Is. 53:9	1 Peter 2:22
Zeal	Ps. 69:9	John 2:17

Parables	Ps. 78:2	Matt. 13, 34–35
Miracles	Is. 35:5–6	Matt. 11:4–6; John 11:47
Reproach	Ps. 22:6; 69:7, 9, 20	Rom. 15:3
Rejected by His own	Ps. 69:8; Is. 63:3	John 1:11; 7:5
Stumbling stone	Is. 8:14	Rom. 9:32; 1 Peter 2:8
Hated	Ps. 35:19–21; 69:4	John 15:24–25
Rejected by leaders	Ps. 118:22	Matt. 21:42; John 7:48
All oppose	Ps. 2:1–2	Luke 23:12; Acts 4:27
Betrayed	Ps. 41:9; 55:12–14	John 13:18, 21
Disciples leave	Zech. 13:7	Matt. 26:31, 56
Sold	Zech. 11:12	Matt. 26:15
Potter's field	Zech. 11:13	Matt. 27:7
Sufferings	Ps. 22:14–15	Luke 22:41, 44
Vicarious sufferings	Is. 53:4–6, 12; Dan. 9:25–27	Matt. 20:28
Patience	Is. 53:7	Matt. 23:37; 27:12–14
Smitten	Micah 5:1	Matt. 27:30
Marred	Is. 52:14; 53:3	John 19:5
Scourged	Is. 50:6	Mark 14:65; John 19:1
Nailed	Ps. 22:16	John 19:18; 20:25
Forsaken by God	Ps. 22:1	Matt. 27:46
Mocked	Ps. 22:7–8	Matt. 27:39–44
Gall	Ps. 69:21	Matt. 27:34
Lots for vesture	Ps. 22:18	Matt. 27:35
With transgressors	Is. 53:12	Mark 15:28
Intercession	Is. 53:12	Luke 23:34
Death	Is. 53:12	Matt. 27:50
No bone broken	Ex. 12:46; Ps. 34:20	John 19:33, 36
Pierced	Zech. 12:10	John 19:34, 37
Burial	Is. 53:9	Matt. 27:57–60
No corruption	Ps. 16:10	Acts 2:31
Resurrection	Ps. 16:10; Is. 26:19	Luke 24:6–7, 31, 34
Ascend	Ps. 68:18	Luke 24:51; Acts 1:9
Right hand of God	Ps. 110:1	Heb. 1:3

The Sermon

Advent unfolds the revelation of Christ and develops thanksgiving for Jesus' coming to save and returning to judge. In this church service we stress preparing the way *with God's prophets.* At Christmas His messengers bring news of a Savior to deliver us from all our enemies. What horror if the news were of a Judge to bring on us more wrath, damnation, and hellfire! Instead, He sends tidings of great joy, not wrath, of peace and goodwill. The angels sing joyfully because God Himself is joyful in all He does and promises us.

Months before the Christmas angels gave the news Zechariah said, "God spoke to our fathers, to Abraham and to his posterity for ever." So also said the blessed virgin Mary, "God spoke by the mouth of His holy prophets."

And what was that message which prompted Mary to say, "My soul magnifies the Lord, and my spirit rejoices in God my Savior," and for Zechariah to speak, "Blessed be the Lord God of Israel, for He has visited and redeemed His people"? Mary says it is "in remembrance of His mercy, as He spoke to our fathers"; Zechariah says it is "as He spoke by the mouth of His holy prophets." Let's begin with the prophets who prepare the way as they encourage us along the way. We can rejoice that God keeps His word.

I. Who Are God's Prophets?

Alexander Cruden explained "Prophets" in his *Concordance* (1737): "Ordinarily this word is understood as meaning one who foretells future events. It meant, at the time our English Bible was translated, also a preacher—and prophesying meant preaching. A meaning of the word less often recognized, but really as common, is one who tells or a forth-teller—who speaks for another, most usually for God. It is in this sense that many Bible characters are called prophets, as, for example, Aaron, Moses, and Jesus Christ."

Prophets are preachers of the word of another. Prophets speak for another, not themselves. God told Moses, "Aaron . . . shall be your prophet"(Ex. 7:1). He spoke for Moses, who was "slow of speech and of tongue" (Ex. 4:10).

Moses himself was a real prophet, for he gave God's words in laws and rules to God's people. He was God's mouthpiece. He once defined a prophet and prophecy this way (Deut. 18:15–22): "The Lord your God will raise up for you a prophet like me from among you. . . . And the Lord said to me . . . 'I will raise for them a prophet like you from among their brethren; and I will put my words in his mouth, and he shall speak to them all that I command him. And whoever will not give heed to my words which he shall speak in my name, I myself will require it of him. But the prophet who presumes to speak a word in my name which I have not commanded him to speak, or who speaks in the name of other gods, that same prophet shall die.' And if you say in your heart, 'How may we know the word which the Lord has not spoken?'—when a prophet speaks in the name of the Lord, if the word does not come to pass or come true, that is a word which the Lord has not spoken; the prophet has spoken it presumptuously, you need not be afraid of him."

This passage about coming prophets New Testament writers applied to Jesus Christ (Act 3:22–23; 7:37). There were many prophets, but one special Prophet was expected.

Ps. 110:4 says that Christ is "a priest forever after the order of Melchizedek." He is our High Priest, and is Himself the last sacrifice. Christ's believers are the new royal priesthood of believers (1 Peter 2:9). "When there is a change in the priesthood, there is necessarily a change in the law" (Heb. 7:12). For example, the sacrifice laws were changed. Christ was God's Lamb to take away the sins of the world. The Law was necessary, but when new revelations came through Jesus Christ, it was as John wrote, "The Law was given through Moses; grace and truth came through Jesus Christ" (John 1:17). The new Prophet, Jesus, was no destroyer of the Law, nor a clone of Moses to teach the Law. He came to fulfill the Law.

Like Moses, He spoke in God's name. He said of Himself (Is. 61:1): "The Spirit of the Lord God is upon me, because the Lord has anointed me to bring good tidings to the afflicted; He has sent me to bind up the broken-hearted, to proclaim liberty to the captives, and the opening of the prison to those who are bound." That was His task.

As the new Prophet He taught what the Father revealed. What He had seen the Father do, or what He heard, this the new Prophet repeated. Whoever despises Him despises the Father who sent Him. All men should honor Him as they honor the Father. What He says of Himself, of His purpose, and of His sacrifice is true, supported by the writings of Law, Prophets, and Psalms and by signs, "that you may know that the Son of Man has authority on earth" (Matt. 9:6). False prophets may come and pretend they are Christ. But these can be tested by God's Word or by signs and be proven false.

II. We See Christ as the True Prophet

Was Jesus just another prophet? No, He was more than a prophet. Was He another king? Not another king, but King of kings. Was He another holy man? No, but the holiest; none could accuse Him of sin.

Tasting rejection, Jesus told the people that "no prophet is acceptable in his own country" (Luke 4:24). But after inspired insight, healings, miracles, and speeches, many acknowledged Him as prophet—the Samaritan woman (John 4:19); the healed blind man telling the Pharisees, "He is a prophet" (John 9:17); Herod suspecting Jesus is John or a prophet come back to life (Luke 9:7–9). After 5,000 ate because of His miracle the crowd said, "This is indeed the prophet who is to come into the world" (John 6:14). In sermons both Peter (Acts 3:22–23) and Stephen (Acts 7:37) applied Moses' words in Deut. 18 to Christ.

Thus with joy we describe Jesus as the Way, and hold in faith His words: "We are going up to Jerusalem; and the Son of Man will be delivered to the chief priests and scribes, and they will condemn Him to death, and deliver Him to the Gentiles; and they will mock Him, and spit upon Him, and scourge Him, and kill Him; and after three days He will rise" (Mark 10:33–34).

III. Other Prophets Predict the Christ

There were many prophets in Israel: women like Deborah (Judg. 4:4), priests like Aaron (Ex. 7:1), kings like David (Acts 2:30), farmers like Amos (Amos 7:14–15). While some wrote books, like Jeremiah (Jer. 30:1), "The word . . . came to Jeremiah from the Lord: 'Thus says the Lord . . . Write in a book all the words that I have spoken to you,' " others, like Elijah, wrote no books but their work was recorded for our learning (1 Kings 17 ff.).

Prophets had strong dialog with people for whom it was clear what God's special message was for each situation. These messages were often given in radical form or "acted out." How clear was the message to the prophet? Amos writes (3:7): "The Lord God does nothing, without revealing His secret to His servants the prophets." Peter adds (1 Peter 1:10–11): "The prophets who prophesied of the grace that was to be yours searched and inquired about this salvation; they inquired what person or time was indicated by the Spirit of Christ within them when predicting the sufferings of Christ and the subsequent glory." Such revelation from God became clear when fulfilled. The test for the prophet was, as Moses said: "Is the man the mouthpiece of God?" Does he speak lies or neglect telling what God has revealed?

When Christ walked with the Emmaus disciples, "Beginning with Moses and all the prophets, He interpreted to them in all the Scriptures the things concerning Himself" (Luke 24:27). After "their eyes were opened" (v. 31), they said, "Did not our hearts burn within us while He talked to us on the road, while He opened to us the Scriptures?" (v. 32).

Extensive lists can be made of prophecies and fulfillment respecting Christ. We gave only some of these in the "Notes" to this chapter.

We in the church are founded on the apostles and prophets, and what they preached and taught is Christ, the Cornerstone on whom our faith rests. "No other foundation can anyone lay than that which is laid, which is Jesus Christ" (1 Cor. 3:11).

Advent 3

Preparing the Way

By Repentance

Matthew 3:2; Mark 1:14–15

Notes

1. Jer. 31:18–19 has Ephraim bemoaning to God, "Thou hast chastened me, and I was chastened, like an untrained calf; bring me back that I may be restored, for Thou art the Lord my God. For after I had turned away I repented; and after I was instructed, I smote upon my thigh; I was ashamed, and I was confounded, because I bore the disgrace of my youth." After punishment from God and *after instruction* Ephraim recognized the wrong, turned from the sin, and turned to God. The rebuke helped Ephraim. The Law does its work, showing us God's wrath. The hand of God does His work, turning us from sin unto Himself. God gives the impetus for both turnings; the acknowledgment of the wrong and renunciation of such sin is what God asks. So then we would pray, "Bring me back that I may be restored." And the way of restoration is by repentance.

2. The Lord delights in repentance because it is proper, leads to hatred of sin, but more to following God. So three parables in Luke 15 (sheep, coin, son) stress His joy over the sinner who repents. In the parable in Matt. 21:28–32 the son who changed his mind is the blessed one. Those who did not repent are rebuked by our Lord. For God has no pleasure in the death of the wicked, but has pleasure in those who repent.

3. *Metanoia* means a change, thus it comes *after* knowledge of Law and Gospel, through God's Word. In pagan circles *metanoia* did not necessarily mean a change for the better. It is the input of Christ which makes all the difference in a *godly repentance.*

The Sermon

As the celebration of Jesus' birth draws closer, make plans to prepare. Primary is His word, "I am the Way ... no one comes to the Father, but by Me" (John 14:6). At Christmas we praise God, who provided that Way and prepared for that Gift by many promises.

To be ready to celebrate His birth we heed Amos' word (4:12) to God's people who must meet Him in punishment for sin: "Prepare to meet your God, O Israel!" We prepare spiritually, looking at our spirit in the light of God's Word. Jesus promised that the Holy Spirit would bring to mind what God said and taught. By hearing, believing, obeying His Word we become ready. Of His many words none is more striking for preparation than "Repent!"

I. Importance of Repentance

John preached repentance before Jesus appeared for Baptism. John said to the crowds who came, "Repent, for the kingdom of heaven is at hand." After He was imprisoned Jesus picked up the same theme, saying, "The time is fulfilled, and the kingdom of God is at hand; repent, and believe in the Gospel."

Jesus said angels rejoice over sinners who repent (Luke 15:10). When Jesus' birth was announced, they called Him "Jesus, for He will save His people from their sins" (Matt. 1:21). It was sin which brought Him to earth and for which He made payment with His life.

Repentance is to turn from sin and turn to God for pardon and power. Such turning can be effected not by man's will or decision, but only by the power of God through the holy Gospel.

Repentance begins with inner grief over breaking God's commandments and incurring His wrath. Such grief is over the sin which caused the Son of God to suffer and die a shameful voluntary death to atone for our wrong-doing. Repentance makes us aware that we not only have hurt and offended God, but by such sin have done wrong to our neighbor, e. g., in the family or at work. Such sorrow includes the pain, misery, and suffering brought upon ourselves because envy, hatred, selfishness, and evil desires have taken control. The wages of all this sin is death—temporal, spiritual, and eternal. In serious words God says unless we repent we shall perish and could be condemned eternally. We imagine we are OK and not as bad as others, living under the impression that, since we have escaped punishment, God does not think our sin so serious.

A report came that by bad luck a building collapsed and some tenants were killed. Did they deserve that stroke of "bad luck" more than others because they were worse sinners? Or did the sin lie with the builder who used shoddy materials? with the workmen who did a slipshod job? with the building inspector who either made a careless inspection or, worse, took a

22

bribe to pass a building he knew to be defective? Who deserved destruction? Jesus said, "I tell you ... unless you repent you will all likewise perish" (Luke 13:3, 5). Because people do not repent, our Lord is disturbed. He "is not slow about His promise [to come again], as some count slowness, but is forbearing ... not wishing that any should perish, but that all should reach repentance" (2 Peter 3:9).

Some would rather not discuss repentance, convinced they have not done serious wrong. Repentance, they seem to think, is reserved for thieves on a cross. They seem to consider Jesus' return for judgment as no more than a scare tactic. But God warns us to be prepared for His coming, so that we will not be found lacking in repentance and faith. He is not playing games with us on such a serious matter.

In a speech outside Athens, Paul talked to leaders of the philosophers' community, something like today's agnostics, who do not know whether or not there is a God. Paul said that often in the past God ignored and passed by false worship, indifference, apathy, but since God in Christ appeared all that is changed. "The times of ignorance God overlooked, but now He commands all men everywhere to repent, because He has fixed a day on which He will judge the world" (Act 17:30–31). Judgment is coming. The King is at the gate! It will not be put off.

II. Proclaimers of Repentance

1. *John the Baptist* said, "Repent, for the kingdom of heaven is at hand" (Matt. 3:2). The evangelist then quotes Is. 40: "The voice of one crying in the wilderness: Prepare the way of the Lord, make His paths straight." The wilderness, where action was not expected, is where the action takes place.

It is more than a haunt of evil spirits or where evil lurks (Mark 1:13). It is where God loved and fed His people with manna and with His laws (Ex. 16, 20; Matt. 14:13–21), for men live on God's Word (Matt. 4:4). There He made the covenant (Ex. 24), there He was tested (Ps. 95:8–11), there Christ was baptized, there He prayed (Luke 5:16), there He was served by angels (Matt. 4:11). There He found the lost, pastured the 99 (Luke 15:4), there, He knew, self-styled Messiahs would appear (Matt. 24:26). He led them in, through, out of the wilderness to the Promised Land. Hosea (2:14) portrays God as taking His beloved there to woo her: "I will allure her, and bring her into the wilderness, and speak tenderly to her."

It is in our wildernesses where God speaks and calls, where, confronted with hunger and temptation, loneliness and fear, our spirits are tested and we want to change our minds and lives to be in tune with His life. It is in the wilderness that John pleads, "Repent, for the kingdom of heaven is at hand." There we find a need for God, for a Savior.

To the wilderness to repent! There John directs us to bring forth fruit that befits repentance—not only to turn from sin and turn to the Lord, but to let the change produce fruits of change. Here sorrow for stealing includes despising it and living honestly. Sorrow for adultery means despising it and living in God's standards of purity. Sorrow for misusing God's name calls us to renounce the sin and to remember His name in prayer and praise.

2. *The Lord Jesus Christ Himself* spoke the same message He gave John and the prophets, saying: "The kingdom of God is at hand; repent, and believe in the Gospel."

When He instructed His disciples before His return to heaven, from whence He came, He included this message, "that repentance and forgiveness of sins should be preached in His name to all nations" (Luke 24:47).

3. *The Apostle Peter* understood this. When tried before Israel's chief council for confessing Jesus as Messiah, Peter's defense included these words: "God exalted Him at His right hand as Leader and Savior, to give repentance to Israel and forgiveness of sins" (Acts 5:31). That for Peter was God's highest gift and enabled people to know God more clearly, to follow Him more nearly. Peter experienced this in his own life.

We cannot forget his Pentecost sermon: "When they heard this they were cut to the heart, and said to Peter and the rest of the apostles, 'Brethren, what shall we do?' And Peter said to them, 'Repent, and be baptized every one of you in the name of Jesus Christ for the forgiveness of your sins; and you shall receive the gift of the Holy Spirit. For the promise is to you and to your children and to all that are far off, everyone whom the Lord our God calls to him' " (Acts 2:37–39).

At Jerusalem he reported his encounter with the Gentile soldier Cornelius: "When they heard this they [the opponents to Gentile ministry] were silenced. And they glorified God, saying, 'Then to the Gentiles also God has granted repentance unto life' " (Acts 11:18).

4. *Paul's experience* was not different from John's or Peter's, nor of the Lord Himself. Paul told Agrippa that he "was not disobedient to the heavenly vision," for wherever he preached—at Damascus, Jerusalem, or in all Judea— it was so that Jew and Gentile "should repent and turn to God and perform deeds worthy of their repentance" (Acts 26:19–20). Paul told the elders of Ephesus: "I did not shrink from declaring to you anything that was profitable,

and teaching you in public and from house to house, testifying both to Jews and to Greeks of repentance to God and of faith in our Lord Jesus Christ" (Acts 20:20–21).

The Lord's teaching, like the apostles' and the baptizer's, linked together repentance and forgiveness, repentance and faith in the Gospel. Repentance leads to Jesus Christ, "the Lamb of God who takes away the sin of the world" (John 1:29). Through Him the world is reconciled to God and we find the Way to the Father.

Our baptism teaches us that by contrition and repentance we should daily drown our old Adam with all its evil lusts. Thus by repentance God helps us change our mind about loving what is evil, so that we come to despise it, ever praising the God who frees us from guilt and shame, judgment and wrath, by the sacrifice of His Son.

Advent 4

Prepare the Way

We Believe and Trust

Luke 1:18, 34

Notes

1. Believers, since they already have faith, do not ask to believe. But they say with the apostles, "Increase our faith!" (Luke 17:5). They are not asking for faith itself, but for a deeper, more trusting, more childlike faith. Faith accomplishes things beyond the normal, such as moving mountains or trees into oceans (v. 6). Godless people do not desire faith.

2. The apostles were not always strong believers, men who never doubted. Consider Peter. He with John came to the open tomb. Peter did not enter at first, but later did. Peter saw the linen cloths, the empty tomb, and wondered; but John, seeing it, believed. Neither of them fully understood the Scriptures that Jesus would rise, but, seeing what Peter saw, John believed (John 20:3–10). Jesus said that even if a person rose from the dead it would not convince those who are determined not to believe. Moses and the prophets should be heard (Luke 16:31). Faith comes by hearing the Word (Rom. 10:17). Were empty linen cloths proof enough for John to believe? There was more, for he heard the claims of Jesus that He was God's Son. Faith is planted, nurtured, and grows through and with God's Word. So Zechariah at first did not trust the angel's word of a child to be born to his wife, but later he could in song bless God about what the prophets said and in regard to the "knowledge of salvation" which his son John the Baptist would bring to Israel (Luke 1:70, 77).

3. Belief is the work of the Holy Spirit (1 Cor. 12:3), not of sight, not of touching a nail-print. Seeing and faith are different, one is physical and the other spiritual. Jesus pointed out that some have eyes and do not see, ears and do not hear, minds and do not understand (John 12:40; Is. 6:9–10). Faith is spiritual, the spirit of man, moved by the Spirit of God through His Word. The Spirit will ask that you use what He has already given you.

4. A gold coin in a child's hand is worth as much as in a champion wrestler's hand. Its value is not in the holder but in itself.

5. Christ knew Peter would deny Him. He prayed that Peter's faith would not fail him (Luke 22:31–32, 34). Weak faith may say, "I believe; help my unbelief!" (Mark 9:24) or "Increase our faith!" (Luke 17:5).

6. Faith prompts us to trust in God and approach Him in prayer. "Such is the confidence that we have through Christ toward God" (2 Cor. 3:4). Again, "In [Christ] we have boldness and confidence of access through our faith in Him" (Eph. 3:12). Again, "Let us draw near with a true heart in full assurance of faith" (Heb. 10:22).

The Sermon

Two families of God help us to prepare the way of the Lord. One family is a husband and wife from the hill country of Judea, near Jerusalem; members of the priest class. Pious and godly, they walk in God's ways. Elderly and living alone, they have no children. One day the husband, Zechariah, went to the temple for his work assignment. It fell to his lot to enter the temple and burn incense at the golden altar of incense for one week. Only once in a man's life was this honor given.

In the temple the angel Gabriel suddenly stood beside him and said, "Your prayer is heard, and your wife Elizabeth will bear you a son, and you shall call his name John. . . . Many will rejoice at his birth . . . and he will be filled with the Holy Spirit . . . and he will go before [the Lord] in the spirit and power of Elijah . . . to make ready . . . a people prepared" (Luke 1:13–17).

Zechariah asked, "How shall I know this? For I am an old man; and my wife is advanced in years."

The angel said, "You will be silent and unable to speak . . . because you did not believe my words." When Zechariah came out to give the blessing, he could not speak. He signaled to the people and they understood that he had had a vision from God.

Three months later in Nazareth in Galilee the same angel Gabriel spoke to a young girl, engaged to marry a local carpenter. Like the other couple, both Mary and Joseph were believers in God, pious and good people. The angel told Mary she would have a child, to be named Jesus. "He will be great, and will be . . . the Son of the Most High; and the Lord God will give to Him the throne of . . . David."

Mary asked, "How shall this be, since I have no husband?"

The angel said, "The Holy Spirit will come upon you . . . overshadow you; therefore the child . . . will be . . . holy, the Son of God." The angel also told

Mary that her aged cousin Elizabeth was with child, she "who was called barren. For with God nothing shall be impossible."

I. These Two Families Help Us Prepare the Way

Their example and work ought to encourage us in belief and trust.

No doubt Elizabeth prayed often. In Hebron, near where she and Zechariah lived, their ancestors Jacob and Leah were buried. She heard about Jacob's first love, Rachel, who died on the way to Bethlehem giving birth to Benjamin. She remembered her complaint to Jacob, "Give me children, or I shall die!" (Gen. 30:1), and his answer, "Am I . . . God, who has withheld [children] from you?" (v. 2). Zechariah knew that his ancestors Abraham and Sarah, buried in Hebron, were childless for many years and that Abraham had prayed (Gen 15), "0 Lord God, what wilt Thou give me, for I continue childless?" (Gen. 15:2). Many were denied such gifts of the Lord (cf. Ps. 128:3).

On the other hand, Joseph and Mary were engaged but kept themselves pure. Mary could not understand how she could have a child. When Joseph later learned she was with child, he was upset.

The two responses focus on two attitudes, belief and trust, important for God's people preparing the way this Advent.

Consider Zechariah's question: "How shall I know this," what sign am I given that this will happen? When God promised a child to Abraham, he laughed (Gen. 17:17). So did Sarah, even though she denied it later (Gen 18:12–15). The time came to test Abraham's faith: "Take your son, your only son Isaac, whom you love, and go to . . . Moriah, and offer him there as a burnt offering" (Gen. 22:2). He believed and trusted God, who said that out of Abraham's seed, by Sarah, He would bless all nations. "He considered that God was able to raise men even from the dead" (Heb. 11:19). James (2:20–23) says that Abraham showed his faith by his works, as trust displayed his faith. Zechariah believed but still wanted some signal for trust. He got it, inability to communicate until the child was born.

Consider Mary. Her child, to be named "Jesus," as told both her and Joseph (Matt. 1:21), was born, fulfilling God's promise and God's plan. Paul says: "Christ Jesus came into the world to save sinners" (1 Tim. 1:15). Mary asked for no sign, yet was given one: Your aged cousin Elizabeth is pregnant.

There are *differences in the two responses.* Zechariah said: No trust until I am sure. Mary said: I do not understand what I hear or how it can happen, but let it be to me according to your word."

Zechariah was no unbeliever. Note that at John's birth no better praise and blessing could be spoken than his (Luke 1:67–79). His attitude is like that of his son, who said: I am not worthy to untie His shoe laces (Luke 3:16).

II. Our Reactions to Their Responses - Belief and Trust

1. *Belief centers in confidence,* accepting with little or no hard evidence. Jesus said it: "Blessed are those who have not seen and yet believe" (John 20:29). The Bible affirms: "Faith is the assurance of things hoped for, the conviction of things not seen" (Heb. 11:1).

A similar desire for a child happened in the time of the Judges. An angel appeared to a man named Manoah and his wife, saying she would bear a child. Then we read: "And Manoah said, 'Now when your words come true, what is to be the boy's manner of life, and what is he to do?' " (Judg. 13:12).

Manoah did not say, "If" your words come true, or "Show me how" they will come true, but "When your words come true . . . " That is confidence—faith that trusts, belief that not only says God answers prayer but is ready to say, "When . . . " "This is the confidence which we have in Him, that if we ask anything according to His will He hears us" (1 John 5:14). "We have boldness and confidence of access through our faith in [Christ]" (Eph. 3:12).

2. *Trust says believe and act.* Mark 9:14–29 has a poignant story that happened right after the Transfiguration. A father who before had asked the disciples to heal his demoniac boy (but they failed) brought him to Jesus. The father asked for His help, "if You can do anything." Jesus replied, "If you can! All things are possible to him who believes." The man said, "I believe; help my unbelief!" The New English Bible puts it this way, "I have faith . . . help me where faith falls short."

Whether Zechariah's faith fell short or not, he was no unbeliever. But it seems he was not ready to trust. The word made no sense to him, for he and his wife were old. There are some things we cannot know or need not know, but only believe. Mary believed and trusted. Faith itself is a miracle that accepts God's Word in trust and then goes on to appropriate action.

Hebrews (10:35, 38) says: "Do not throw away your confidence, which has a great reward . . . my righteous one shall live by faith."

Christmas Eve

Prepare the Way

Celebrating Jesus Christ as the Way

Luke 2:10–11; John 14:6

Notes

1. Concerning Christmas *hymns* see note on Christmas Day. The divine presence in the Christ Child is stressed in the Christmas evening hymns.

2. We celebrate Christmas, not "keep" it as the Sabbath, nor "do" it as a task. We celebrate it publicly, expressing joy and accomplishment. Paul either wrote the following himself or got it from an ancient creedal hymn: "Great indeed, we confess, is the mystery of our religion: He was manifested in the flesh, vindicated in the Spirit, seen by angels, preached among the nations, believed on in the world, taken up in glory" (1 Tim. 3:16), and that is the thrust of our texts.

This is the secret which produces godliness or piety within believers. The meaning of *phaneroo* is "lay bare, uncover, reveal, manifest, appear." The word is used for His first coming (1 Tim. 3:16; Heb. 9:26; 1 Peter 1:20; 1 John 1:2) and His appearance on the Last Day (Col. 3:4; 1 Peter 5:41; 1 John 3:2). It has this ingredient, that Christ is real, not hidden, not in a false or pretended guise, but in His true character, as He is, disclosing Himself as He is.

This never happened before in the world's history and will never happen again, that God appeared as a baby among us. His coming is not a division of the world's time schedule into BCE, that is, "Before the Common Era," or CE, "Common Era," as Israel marks its calendar. It is BC, "Before Christ," and AD, "Anno Domini"—"in the year of our Lord." God intersected the straight line of time and Himself made that division by His appearance.

Indeed, the Incarnation is a mystery into which we cannot pry with our reason, but with Paul and the other apostles we say, "Great is the mystery!" Because of His humanity our flesh is in glory at the Father's right hand. He did not change His deity to humanity, nor did He bring His humanity from heaven, but assumed it by conception of the Holy Spirit in the virgin Mary. He is true God and true man. Thus it is proper to say He is eternal God and yet was born on Christmas.

3. The Apostles' Creed says, " . . . who was conceived by the Holy Spirit, born of the Virgin Mary." The Creed of Nicaea says, " . . . who for us men and for our salvation came down from heaven and was incarnate by the Holy Spirit of the virgin Mary and was made man." The Athanasian Creed says " . . . our Lord Jesus Christ, the Son of God, is God and man . . . one Christ . . . not by conversion of the Godhead into flesh but by taking the manhood into God" (quoted from *Lutheran Worship*).

4. Services have taken on customs adding to celebration, such as the candlelight singing of "Silent Night." At one church all faced the center aisle while singing by candlelight, and so the entire congregation could appreciate the candlelight phenomena. People took home their candles and there lit them, reminding each other of Christ, the Light of the world. At a children's manger-scene tableau the pastor knelt with the child participants and there said his *ex corde* prayer.

The Sermon

At Christmas we adore the Christ Child as did angels and shepherds. When Mary visited Elizabeth, the latter said that John leaped in her womb as in joy and adoration for the Child when Mary greeted her (Luke 1:44).

At Christmas we worship as did the Magi (Matt. 2). Herod asked the Wise Men to help him worship this Child, yet his later actions said, "Not so."

At Christmas we rejoice as angels bring good news and the heavens echo the Child's praises. Simeon saw the Child and blessed Him, for he saw Israel's Glory and the Gentiles' Light. Anna gave thanks with joy for His planned redemption.

At Christmas we honor as Lord and God Him whom the Father honored at His baptism and transfiguration, and in His miracles and resurrection. The Father's words, "This is My beloved Son," were known by Satan (Luke 4:3), whose works the Son came to destroy (1 John 3:8).

At Christmas we wonder, "What manner of Child is this?" as the disciples wondered, "What sort of man is this, that even wind and sea obey Him?" (Matt. 8:27).

I. Today We Celebrate Him Who Is the Way

At Christmas we celebrate. Carols echo in marketplace and church, and folks long for peace and goodwill, care about hunger and want, seek relief from evil and wrong, and hunger for righteousness and dignity. All this exhibits a prodigal world wanting to return to the Father's home. Jesus said, "I am the Way, and the Truth, and the Life; no one comes to the Father, but by Me." He is Truth and Life in power and love.

The early Christians were known as followers of "the Way." They believed and confessed the Babe of Bethlehem, crucified in Jerusalem, risen from the dead, as the Way, the answer to men's needs. There was salvation in no one else (Acts 4:12). It was such people whom Paul, before his conversion, wanted to drag to Jerusalem for punishment. Jesus Himself interrupted Paul's desire, informing him whom he was really persecuting: "I am Jesus, whom you are persecuting" (Acts 9:1–5).

Later, across the Aegean Sea at Ephesus, there was "no little stir" when leaders of the idol-making industry complained to the town clerk that their livelihood was being ruined by followers of "the Way" (Acts 19:23–41).

This only Way, Jesus, conceived in Nazareth, whose birth in Bethlehem we celebrate this evening, is, as Simeon said, "set for the fall and rising of many in Israel" (Luke 2:34). This is He whom angels announced as Christ, Lord and Savior, promised by the Father ages ago.

It is a long road from angels bearing a flaming sword of judgment against our first parents to angels announcing good news for all people at Bethlehem, from angels ministering to us night and day as God's servants to the harvest gathered at Judgment Day by angels who work as reapers. But it is a path, a road, a way, a highway across nations and islands, continents and oceans, trod by prophets, by Wise Men, by shepherds, by Mary and Joseph, by prophets, by a sackcloth-garmented figure calling to repentance, by saints and bloodstained martyrs, by pastors and teachers preparing the way for us to meet the Lord, Himself the Way, and have Him here this moment, this night, "where two or three are gathered in [His] name" (Matt. 18:20).

II. Knowing the Way, We Celebrate

What if there were no way back to the Father? Would God be hidden? Would we find Him? Would He find us? What kind of images could we possibly make of Him, using our wildest imagination as to what He might be like? Would we be forever doomed and lost? Would there be anything to celebrate?

Some images on faraway temples depict God as knowing only sex and orgies. Some images, now resting in museums, make Him cruel and angry —a god who needs to be appeased with human sacrifices. Some images, especially those taught in tales and myths of literature from a golden age of the past, make gods "more human than we," full of lust, envy, and anger, schemers of evil, thieves, liars, and weaklings.

Others cry, "It is impossible to know the way to God or God's way to man, for even those who offer themselves as guides prove contradictory or unfaithful to much that is decent and honorable."

The best of humans are imperfect. This year's graduating class will be no better than last year's "class of distinction." We've inherited our past and fail to improve. "There is none that does good, no, not one," cried prophets centuries ago. Were they alive today, they would read again from their own writings: "They have all gone astray, they are all alike corrupt" (Ps. 14:3; Rom. 3:12). Were you to choose the most holy and pious from among your kinsfolk, they would be the first to call themselves, like Paul, "the foremost of sinners" (1 Tim. 1:15).

Even the first human couple, made in God's image, could not be saved on their own. They would have rejoiced tonight to hear the angels announce, "I bring you good news of . . . a Savior, who is Christ the Lord," rather than the angel he saw in Eden guarding with flaming sword the way to the tree of life.

Were we to appeal to father Abraham, "the friend of God" (James 2:23), to intercede for us, we would see one like us, impatient and seeking to get his own way to have a child, or lying and teaching his wife the same to protect himself. Were we to ask Moses to intercede for us, because he was known as the meekest man on earth (Num. 12:3) and the one man with whom God talked face to face (Ex. 33:11), we would see him as one who was denied life in the Promised Land because of his anger. And what of David, the man after God's own heart (1 Sam. 13:14), victim of his own lust and scheming in adultery, lying, and murder?

Why go on? Why name others? Why dig up more dirt? We could not seriously offer either ourselves or any of these people as a possible way to God. They, as we, were people for whom God came. They, too, would celebrate tonight because there is a way. Welcome, blessed angels who sing of the Savior's birth! The plain fact is that none of the greatest of God's workers from the past nor from among us could redeem himself or another (Ps. 49:7–8).

If it were possible, imagine the schemes and plans we would create to gain the favor of such a person. The offerings we would give in return for some assistance, the persuasions we would attempt in an effort to use their goodness to have God on our side! We read how one of Job's friends remarked, "The Almighty—we cannot find Him; He is great in power and justice, and abundant righteousness He will not violate. Therefore men fear Him; He does not regard any who are wise in their own conceit" (Job 37:23–24). On Mars' Hill Paul talked of men who seek Him hoping to find Him (Acts 17:27). But, as He said, God has never been seen nor indeed can be seen (1 Tim. 6:16).

This Christmas Eve we celebrate that our God came in the flesh. Tonight God gives a special sign, "Behold, a virgin shall conceive and bear a Son, and His name shall be called Emmanuel (which means, God with us)" (Matt. 1:23, quoting Is. 7:14).

Mary deserves a special place in our heart. As Elizabeth said, she was "blessed . . . among women" (Luke 1:42). She had willingly consented to become the instrument of the Lord: "Behold I am the handmaid of the Lord; let it be to me according to your [the angel's] word" (v. 38). Her spirit rejoiced in God her Savior (v. 47).

Joseph, her husband, wondered, and when assured he celebrated by providing his best for mother and Child.

Of the Child the prophet said: "To us a Child is born, to us a Son is given; and the government will be upon His shoulder, and His name will be called 'Wonderful Counselor, Mighty God, Everlasting Father, Prince of Peace' " (Is. 9:6).

Jesus Himself in one of His prayers gives us a strong clue for celebration: "This is eternal life, that they know Thee the only true God, and Jesus Christ whom Thou hast sent" (John 17:3). That is why we celebrate.

III. Celebrating Jesus as the Way

Moses asked God, "What is [your] name?" Name? "I AM WHO I AM. . . . Say this to the people . . . 'I AM has sent me' " (Ex. 3:13–14). Besides Him there is none other. He is God of all gods, Lord of all lords. "I AM" was a comfort for Moses.

When some had been concerned about eating, Jesus said: "I am the Bread of life" (John 6:48). Amazed at a blind man seeing, the people heard Jesus say: "I am the Light of the world" (John 8:12). When speaking of His sheep, Jesus said: "I am the Door of the sheep," enter by Me, the Door, and be saved; and, "I am the Good Shepherd," who "lays down His life for the sheep" (John 10:7–11). To a woman mourning the death of her brother He said: "I am the Resurrection and the Life; he who believes in Me . . . shall never die" (John 11:25–26). To His disciples He said: "I am the Vine, you are the branches"—with Me you have life, and so you need to be in the Vine. To churches and their pastors He promised: "I am the Alpha and the Omega," I have the keys of life and death (Rev. 1:8, 18). To churches under the persecution of Caesar, in an empire hostile to the King of kings and His followers, He said: "I am the Root and the Offspring of David, the bright Morning Star" (Rev. 22:16).

To each He gives the appropriate message. To God's followers, His children who ask and hope, ready to celebrate the road back to God and road from God to them, He speaks as to Thomas: "I AM *the Way,* and the Truth, and the Life; no one comes to the Father, but by Me" (John 14:6).

Christmas Day

Prepare the Way

Rejoicing in the Way

Luke 2:10–11, 20

Notes

1. A cursory review of Christmas hymns in three hymnals used by Lutheran churches shows a majority of the hymns with references to Christmas Day deal with rejoicing and the deity of Jesus Christ, while hymns with references to Christmas Eve or Night deal with the divine presence. This prompted the separation of thought between Christmas Eve and Christmas Day in this series.

2. The note of joy is prominent in Christmas Day's text (Luke 2:10–11, 20). While the joy of the wicked is derived from earthly pleasures (Eccl. 2:4–11) and folly (Prov. 15:21), for them it is delusive (Prov. 14:13) and short-lived (Job 20:12–15; Eccl. 7:6) and shall be turned into mourning (James 4:9). Real joy is a gift of God (Ps. 4:7; Eccl. 2:26) through the Holy Spirit (Gal. 5:22). It is prepared for God's people (Ps. 97:11), promised to them (Ps. 132:16; Is. 35:10), and experienced by them (Luke 24:52). The Gospel, announced at Christmas, is the source of our joy (Luke 2:10–11). Joy is associated with temporal blessings (Joel 2:23–24), divine protection (Ps. 5:11; 16:8–9), divine support (Ps. 28:7; 63:7), and victory in Christ (John 16:33). It is expressed in hymns (Eph. 5:19; James 5:13), enjoyed under calamities (Hab. 3:17–18) and persecutions (Matt. 5:11–12; Luke 6:22–23), experienced in sorrow (2 Cor. 6:10) and affliction (Ps. 30:5; 126:5; Is. 35:10). Our joy is that because of Christ our names are written in heaven (Luke 10:20). Our source and strength is in the angels' tidings of great joy.

3. The *Gloria in Excelsis* finds its best commentary in Ps. 147–150. The glory theme is woven into the Lukan narrative. Look up Luke 4:15; 5:25–26; 7:16; 13:13; 17:15, 18; 18:43; 19:38; 21:27; 23:47; 24:26. About the phrase in Luke 2:14, "with whom He is pleased," look up Ps. 149:4.

4. To celebrate the Christmas Gospel, read it in drama form, printed out. This is effective for participation, sharing, and edification. Certain segments

of the audience read the shepherds' part; others, Mary's words; some, those of the Magi; still others, those of the scribes. Participation in sharing parts of the hymn-singing (rather than a choral concert or massive production involving children and youth) adds to the festive, joyful spirit. The Gospel brings joy without adding burdensome rehearsals in the already-too-busy Advent season. It is also unnecessary to add symbolism such as burning incense or weighing out coins of gold. Responsive liturgies, spoken or sung, differing from the "regular" service, can be created quickly and readily. College students, home for the holidays, may well want to join in planning these festivities.

The Sermon

It is nothing new to tell you that Christmas is a time to celebrate. The world does not hesitate to give its help so you can feast, sing, play, drink, give parties. But it will work doubly hard to keep Christ from "spoiling" the Christmas celebration and support all efforts to keep separate church and state, church and business, church and school, church and family. They do not want any religious influence in the celebration. "What's Christ got to do with Christmas?" is their view.

Should a child of God fight the world and its ways or discover that in our faith—not in laws or ordinances—there is a "victory that overcomes the world" (1 John 5:4)? We recognize there will be persecution, but we turn the other cheek, carry on, train our family, find strength in our Lord, serve and share wherever we can, attend our gatherings, and support the causes that promote the teachings of our Lord.

The world cannot celebrate something it does not know. They have eyes but do not see, ears but do not hear, minds but do not understand (cf. Is. 10; Mark 8:18). Spiritual matters can be understood only by spiritual people (1 Cor. 2:12–15). To enrich ourselves in the Spirit, to search our own hearts by the power of the Spirit, to find spiritual strength in the Word and the Sacrament, to praise God for His gifts of grace, to pray that He would give His strength to all who know Him, to pray for those who know Him not and ask God to use us in His way to bring them our hope in Christ, and always to be ready "to make a defense ... for the hope that is in [us]" (1 Peter 3:15)—such is the path we tread these days.

I. We Rejoice to Know the Way in Christ
The Book of Acts relates much effort to proclaim Jesus' coming in the flesh.

It refers to the Christian faith as "the Way" (16:17; 18:26; 19:9, 23; 24:14). Christians recognized the death and resurrection of Jesus as the way to obtain forgiveness of sins, the way to eternal salvation for the whole world, through the Messiah.

Normally the word "way" has different meanings. It could be a road (like the way to Bethlehem), or a highway through the desert (for travelers or exiles to come home), or the road back to God (such as the prodigal son took, requiring repentance and forgiveness). It is in reference to this spiritual path that Jesus called Himself "the Way," saying: "I am the Way, and the Truth, and the Life; no one comes to the Father, but by Me" (John 14:6).

Mary and Joseph's trip from Nazareth to Bethlehem was neither easy nor joyful, for Mary was pregnant and the almost-100-mile trip took place during the national census, when many families were required to return to their ancestral hometown. Many pilgrims were on the roads.

There were also many Roman soldiers. In the comparatively small province of Syria were four legions, or more than 10,000 soldiers, policing Syria, Lebanon, and Palestine, Rome's number-one trouble spot. All of Spain required three and Egypt two legions, but Syria needed four. The unrest and police-state atmosphere made the trip uncomfortable. Pious Jews nearing Bethlehem thought of another trip, one that took place more than a thousand years before. Jacob and his family were returning to settle in Canaan. After giving birth to her husband Jacob's baby, Benjamin, Rachel died. Jacob never forgot that and commented on it as he was dying in Egypt (Gen. 48:7). Many centuries later the Babylonians conquered Palestine and carried into slavery thousands of young people. In their grief people said that in her grave "Rachel is weeping for her children; she refuses to be comforted ... because they are not" (Jer. 31:15).

Matthew heard Rachel's voice once more when Herod slaughtered the innocents at Bethlehem (2:17–18).

Now Rachel's descendants (as well as all of Jacob's) are being numbered in a Roman census. Rome wanted to know how many soldiers were required to control the area and if taxes should be increased. Neither Rome nor Palestine knew that traveling to Bethlehem those days was the Almighty Lord Himself, who came to destroy all works of Satan and save all, whether Jew or Babylonian or Roman.

For all of us there are dangers, emergencies, the unknown, unrest, upsetting situations, and enemies lurking behind the turns in our way of life. It is an inner joy which none can take from us to know that God is at hand,

God is in control, God guides the situations of life. Yet all things work together for good to those who love God (Rom. 8:28), who know the way in Christ (John 14:4). We do not know what lies ahead on our path of life, but we need to ask only if we know Christ, the Way. The King of kings and Lord of lords is on the path we walk. He is by our side, and has prepared the way ahead of us.

To find lodging in little Bethlehem had always been a problem, but now it was confusion. Those who had left the family homestead during the previous 10 years to seek work and fortune were coming home. The town was overrun with pilgrims. There was little room for travelers. The place where animals fed was the only shelter available. The Lord whom the heavens cannot contain (1 Kings 8:27) appeared in the flesh (John 1:14) and is laid in a manger.

But God provides, perhaps not always what we prefer. If we have prayed and this is all He provides, then that is under His care and on His way. God has gone ahead and seen to it that something is there. The little with God is far better than the much without Him. Proverbs (15:17) says it is better to have a soup of garden herbs and eat it in peace with God and among friends than to have a feast and eat it in bitterness and hatred. "There is great gain in godliness with contentment; for we brought nothing into the world, and we cannot take anything out of the world" (1 Tim. 6:6–7). Often the poor of this world know His care more than the wealthy. But whether wealthy or poor, God be praised if we know Him and His care!

The Child was born, of whom Mary wondered how He would be conceived. The Boy was born whom Joseph was to name Jesus because He would save people from their sins, but who made Joseph wonder whether or not to continue with the marriage. Both Mary and Joseph meditated, trusted, and relied on the promises of God. Both rejoiced in the news the shepherds shared with them about the angels' message.

When the way gets rough with doubt or bewilderment, when the unknown becomes unbearable, when we wonder if there is any way to resolve our difficulty, how good to know and rejoice that we know the way in Christ!

Joseph and Mary trusted and supported each other, for when Christ literally and spiritually was in their midst they had a presence and power which is also ours to keep us together with God and one another. The home centers around Him. "Unless the Lord builds the house, those who build it labor in vain" (Ps. 127:1). The presence of God—what a joy to know Him!

Christ vested Himself in our nature. He took our humanhood unto Himself and was born of a virgin. He willingly humbled Himself as a servant and took our place. He died for all, even the ungodly (Rom. 5:6–10).

II. We Celebrate that We Know Him and Pray that Others Find Joy Through Us

Our joy today is more than that Mary had a safe delivery or that a baby was born. Our Lord once commented, "When a woman is in travail she has sorrow, because her hour has come; but when she is delivered of the child, she no longer remembers the anguish, for joy that a child is born into the world" (John 16:21). Joy belongs with the birth of a child. The fruit of the womb is God's reward. But this was more. This was extraordinary. There were heavenly messengers from God. There was a message of hope, of peace, of salvation, of forgiveness, a message which could come only from heaven itself. When hearing it the shepherds without hesitation went to Bethlehem. This was the birth of One to be Savior of the world. This was One who is Christ, that is, the Anointed One, the Promised One. This was not only a boy, a man, but the Lord, God in the flesh. The Lord had donned the vesture of humanity. The Infinite came as an infant. He who is spirit came in flesh.

To know Him is to know eternal life and the way to it (John 17:3). To know Him is to know the Father and the way to Him (John 14:9). To know Him is to be able to come into the very presence of the Holy One, the Creator and Sustainer of this world and all that there is in worlds not yet known to man. To know Him is to be persuaded that He will keep our very life committed unto Him until the Day of Judgment (cf. 2 Tim. 1:12).

It is such knowledge that gives the hope and continuing joy which God freely and willingly shares with us as pilgrims, travelers along life's way, needing rest amid our restlessness, faith when our faith falls short, hope when all is despair, light when all is gloom, confidence when doubts jump from the hidden corners of our heart demanding answers. God in Christ comes to us, who are weary and worn, tired and tried, sinning and making mistakes, forgiving all our sins, so we can lift up our heads and rejoice with the shepherds and Mary, Joseph and the Wise Men. Will it ever happen that we will find joy along the journey of life? Yes! He came; it happened!

Some have lost that joy, as Jesus said, because of persecution or troubles, and the seed of the Word could not take deep root, and the joy was lost (Mark 4:16–17). Some have lost the joy because, like the rich young ruler, they wanted to follow Him but left in sorrow, for they had other loves (Mark

10:22). For all such we pray that with us they can celebrate in knowing Him. This joy God wants them to have: joy in knowing the Lord cares, in knowing the Lord is present, in knowing God forgives mistakes, in knowing He casts no one aside.

The shepherds "made known the saying which had been told them concerning this Child; and all who heard it wondered at what the shepherds told them" (Luke 2:17–18). As we celebrate knowing Him, we too share with those who know Him not.

New Year's Eve

Prepare the Way

Memories of His Mercies

Luke 1:67–75

Notes

1. The *Benedictus* is text material for both New Year's Eve and New Year's Day, using the first section for ending the year of mercies and the second section for future guidance (most commentaries make a threefold division). This song is like Mary's *Magnificat* in that it embraces many Old Testament references, the *Magnificat* using more passages from the Psalms and the *Benedictus* using more from prophecies. References in the *Benedictus* include Ps. 41:13; 72:18–19; 106:48; 111:9; 132:17; Ezek. 29:21; 1 Sam. 2:10; Ps. 106:10; Gen. 22:16; Ex. 2:24; Ps. 105:8–9; 106:45; Jer. 11:5; Micah 7:20; Mal 3:1; Is. 40:3; 42:7; 9:2; Ps. 107:10.

It is called a prophecy (Luke 1:67). The author, Zechariah, comes from a prominent family within the priesthood class, namely Abijah (Luke 1:5), a priest who returned to Jerusalem with Zerubbabel (Neh. 12:1, 4, 17). One author says it is the "last prophecy of the old dispensation and the first of the new, thus forming the link between the two." It has been used in public worship since about A. D. 500.

2. Some call this evening Sylvester Eve, remembering the traditional date for the death of Pope Sylvester (A. D. 335), who received the Donation of Constantine.

Others call it "Watch Night," watching and waiting for the New Year to come, praying in the Lord's house in the company of spiritually minded folks, acting out the admonition to be "awake when He comes" (Luke 12:35–40). Nonliturgical folks omit the New Year's Day celebration but spend much effort and time in separating themselves from the world by providing appropriate movies, meals, meditations, and mementos for the faithful. How good to do both!

3. The influence of Holy Scripture in the canticles is no accident, nor a skillfully crafted creation. Although the printing press had not been invented, the Word was well known to God's people from the readings in the syn-

agogues, the instruction of teachers, and conversations within the family circle. There is a similarity to the way our catechism and hymnal use the Bible, but the canticles are much richer in their use of the primary texts.

To interpret and understand the *Benedictus* and similar writings takes great familiarity with God's Word, an art not found among Christians as frequently as it should be. Paul encouraged Timothy: "Continue in what you have learned and have firmly believed, knowing from whom you learned it and how from childhood you have been acquainted with the sacred writings which are able to instruct you for salvation through faith in Christ Jesus" (2 Tim. 3:14–15).

4. Symbolism and language are very expressive in the *Benedictus*— there is *visitation* by God, coupled with *redemption.* A *born* of salvation is spoken of *by the mouth* of the prophets. There is a *holy covenant and oath* coupled with *swearing* by God. Those who *sit in darkness* and in *death's shadow* find light *dawning* upon them. All these are loaded with Old Testament references.

The *born* was considered a symbol of strength, such as an animal would have. Michelangelo's large statue of Moses in the chapel of St. Peter in Chains in Rome clearly indicates Moses' strength with horns. In Ps. 18:1 God is "the horn of my salvation." Christ, God's Lamb, had seven horns, demonstrating power (Rev. 5:6). The wicked have power like "the horns of the wild oxen" (Ps. 22:21).

The Sermon

> We gather up in this brief hour
> The mem'ry of Thy mercies:
> Thy wondrous goodness, love, and pow'r
> Our grateful song rehearses.

I. What Does It Mean to Bless?

"What part of our church services do you like the best?" the pastor asked his catechumen class. One boy answered, "The benediction." Others laughed. One agreed, saying, "Yes, that's the best part, because church is over." When the boy was asked to explain his answer he said, "After everything has been said and sung, and after I've finished my own thinking, and after all have done their job, it's nice to hear the benediction like a good word from God." That's it, to bless is to say a good word! Here are *three samples of a blessing.*

Esau asked his father Isaac, "Have you but one blessing, my father? Bless me . . . also" (Gen. 27:38). So Isaac gave Esau a good word too, a benediction, but not as rich a one as he had given his brother Jacob.

Another: *Noah's son Ham* mocked his father sleeping off heavy wine-bibbing. Noah's two other boys covered their father's nakedness. When Noah awoke and saw what had happened, he said to the two, "Blessed . . . be Shem . . . God enlarge Japheth," but for the third son, Ham, he had no "good word" (Gen. 9:25–27).

Again: When *Abram* defeated four kings to rescue his nephew Lot, who had been taken prisoner, *Melchizedek,* king of Salem, blessed him. "Blessed be Abram by God Most High, and blessed be God Most High . . . " he said. "And Abram gave him a tenth of everything" (Gen. 14:18–20). Consider our text. Not having children, the priest Zechariah and his wife Elizabeth prayed often for a child. Then one day, when Zechariah was serving at the altar, God told him by an angel that his wife would have a child, a boy, who was to be named John. The joy would be doubled because this boy in manhood would prepare people for the coming of the Savior. Questioning the announcement, Zechariah was struck with loss of speech. When the boy was born, there was much joy. And as soon as he was named "John," Zechariah, with tongue loosed, said a strong good word about God and about the child.

Zechariah blessed God, first, for visiting and redeeming His people, and second, for giving him a boy who would announce the coming of the Savior. His benediction gives more thanks for salvation than for the baby. That was typical of this family, more interested in praising God than self. Later John said it thus: "He [Jesus] must increase, but I must decrease" (John 3:30).

You might say it's typical of priests to praise God and say a good word, a blessing, for Him. Moses' father-in-law was a non-Jewish priest of Midian. When he visited Moses in the Sinai desert, he said to him: "Blessed be the Lord, who has delivered you out of the hand of the Egyptians and . . . of Pharaoh" (Ex. 18:10).

Blessing God is not only for priests. For opportunity to initiate and support building the temple, *David* was grateful and said so; besides, he asked the people to show gratitude, saying (1 Chron. 29:10, 20): "Blessed art Thou, O Lord, the God of Israel our father, forever and ever" and "to all the assembly, 'Bless the Lord your God.' " And they did.

In a time of disaster *Job* spoke a good word even after losing children, produce, and cattle. You may remember his words (1:21): "The Lord gave, and the Lord has taken away; blessed be the name of the Lord."

We are encouraged throughout the Bible to give thanks, to praise, to speak the good word. The Book of Psalms has many prayers, some complaints or questions, but all the divisions in the psalter end with almost the same good words: "Blessed be the Lord, the God of Israel, from everlasting to everlasting! Amen and amen" (Ps. 41:13).

Coming to the end of our year, we proclaim a good word. Should we say, "Blessings, we balanced the books!"? Should we hope God says to us, "Good job! Well done!"? Good, but not everyone ends the year that way. The year may end in success or failure, health or sickness, family or empty nest, another wedding anniversary or loneliness, passing grades or repeating a class. Tonight, like Zechariah, we say with the psalmist (72:18): "Blessed be the Lord, the God of Israel, who alone does wondrous things. Blessed be His glorious name forever; may His glory fill the whole earth! Amen and Amen!"

The liturgical ending of our service is a model to follow. The pastor calls out, "Bless we the Lord," and the people say, "Thanks be to God!" Visiting a campus chapel for a service, I was impressed with the way the students in united voice shouted that response. That is what the benediction, the blessing, the good word, is; it is a word of thanks to God, which we think about so strongly that all should hear what we affirm. God is Lord, and our enemies are defeated. The Lord is our God, and we are His children.

II. Why Do We Bless God?

Why should we say a good word for God? Don't we have something to do with our success? Ask Zechariah. From the text we know why Zechariah blessed God. God honored him and his wife with a child in answer to their prayers. They had no other means to get one. Only God could give it, and when you ask God for a gift of His love and you see His kindness, your heart is full of joy.

We try our best and work hard. But "unless the Lord builds the house, those who build it labor in vain" (Ps. 127:1). God must put a good word on our efforts. Without Him nothing is possible; with Him all is possible.

Again, God's people of old waited long for a Savior. Their worship, sacrifices, diet, and social barriers pointed to a Messiah who was to come. It was like the shadow of a person they could not see but who was now about to be revealed (Col. 2:17). Here the parents are given a special child who

46

is to prepare the way for the promised Messiah and bring to light Him who was in the dark, who seemed to hide. What they said was impossible God made possible. With a loosened tongue, prompted by the Holy Spirit, Zechariah sang out: "Blessed be the Lord, the God of Israel!" Why? God has redeemed us from sin and damnation in Christ, a redemption we could never have accomplished or even approached.

God gives us good words, benedictions. His Book is filled with them. Like in a treasure-house we explore and are surprised by the new treasures. We become like birds that harvest the seeds and good grain which God provides.

God spoke specifically and directly to Zechariah. Would He do so for me? He could, "For with God nothing will be impossible" (Luke 1:37). But will He? God has already given us guidance, promises, revelation in Scripture. The question might be rephrased, "Has God spoken to me as He did to Zechariah with words of blessing and promise?" The answer is yes—through Scripture. Believers listen to Jesus saying, "If you continue in My word, you are truly My disciples, and you will know the truth, and the truth will make you free" (John 8:31–32).

Zechariah was reassured. Prophets of old predicted the coming of a Messiah and His forerunner. As Zechariah said in his good word, his child would be part of God's benediction. Any immediate, extraordinary revelation could never contradict, alter, or add to what already was "inspired by God and profitable ... that the man of God may be complete, equipped for every good work" (2 Tim. 3:16–17).

While it was not first on Zechariah's list, it could well be on ours tonight, that we thank Him for the *gift of life* and all that sustains it. Jesus is our Life; in Him is life (John 1:4). He is the Blessed One, "the blessed and only Sovereign, the King of kings and Lord of lords" (1 Tim. 6:15).

Take comfort, friend; your life is not unknown to the Lord. Ps. 139 expresses it well. The Lord has searched and known you. He knows when you sit down and when you rise up. He discerns your thoughts. He is acquainted with all your ways (vv. 1–3). That is why you can begin every new year with joy, and every month and every week and every day and every moment.

New Year's Day

Prepare the Way

For Our Future

Luke 1:76–79

Notes

1. See comments on "Benedictus" (Luke 1:68–79) under New Year's Eve, since it is the text for New Year's Eve and New Year's Day, its first part dealing with the past (New Year's Eve) and the second with the future (New Year's Day).

2. Installation of Church Council at the service is good timing. Often some suggest it be postponed or predated to avoid the New Year's small attendance. Such suggestions could easily be discouraging, for the very suggestion indicates what value some place on the New Year's Day services. Holy Communion fits in well.

Some parishes have a luncheon after the service for "retiring" officers and those newly installed. If possible, include the whole family, for they are proud of their family member chosen to aid the pastor in ministry. A good word of thanks and commendation needs be paid all these workers. This might be a good time to bring in a district or synodical person to speak of the total work of the church or to have a layman address the luncheon on "Serving the Lord."

3. Sources inform us that the Romans honored this day the two-headed god Janus, the god of "beginnings," both temporal and spatial. As spatial god he presided over gates and doors; as temporal god, over the first hour of the day, the first day of the month, and the first month of the year (named for him). He was represented with two bearded heads set back to back. Because of His strong influence, Christians pointed to Jesus as Beginning and End, Alpha and Omega. The name of Jesus was promoted over that of Janus.

When was Jesus named? At His circumcision, when eight days old. The octave would begin with Dec. 25, which eventually became Christmas. This fit in with the Dec 22 winter solstice, when the sun begins its journey back north, which the Romans celebrated with their "Saturnalia." As the daylight returns, freeing us from the darkness of winter, so Christ, "the Light of the world" (John 8:12), brings spiritual light into the darkness of this world. Surely, picking this time for Christmas was not accommodation but using Roman culture to contrast and illustrate the truths of God.

4. The ordering of redemption in the second part of Zechariah's song has (1) knowledge of salvation; (2) forgiveness of sins; (3) tender mercy of God; (4) giving light (epiphanying in darkness and death); (5) guidance in the way of peace.

Our walk is in "the way of peace" (v. 79b). It is this Christian walk, so in contrast to the world's ways, which is noticed especially by those who know not Christ. The light of Christ (v. 79a) guides the individual Christian and the Christian community on its pilgrimage (Ps. 119:105). Where begin or continue our service for the Lord but with "knowledge of salvation" (v. 77)? What is the source of our strength but God's "tender mercy" (v. 78)?

The Sermon

Today is eight days after Jesus' birth, remembered by the church as the day Jesus was named, although His name was revealed to Mary at the Annunciation (Luke 1:31) and to Joseph when he learned she was with child (Matt. 1:21). His name was to be Jesus because, "He will save His people from their sins" (Matt. 1:21).

Boys at Jesus' time were circumcised on their eighth day. Some suggest it was because eight people were saved in Noah's ark, but that symbolism is more fitting in Christian baptism (1 Peter 3:20–21). At the circumcision the boy was given his Hebrew name, indicating that he is not only a physical son but also a spiritual son of Abraham (Deut. 10:16).

"Jesus" was no new Hebrew name. It is Greek for "Joshua" or "Yeshua," meaning "Jehovah is salvation." Joshua a well-known Hebrew, of the tribe of Ephraim (Num. 13:8, 16), was attendant to Moses and later let the Israelites in the conquest of the Promised Land. He had a strong, positive faith (Num. 14:6–9; Joshua 24:15).

At John's circumcision the relatives wanted to name him Zechariah after his father. His mother protested, "Not so; he shall be called John." They were all surprised, for no one in the family was named John, meaning, "Jehovah is gracious." The relatives turned to the boy's father, muted for nearly a year, and he wrote on a writing tablet: "His name is John." As he was writing, his tongue was unloosed and he spoke quite freely, blessing God for all He was doing, and talking about a new day of forgiveness. Zechariah's words gushed from his mouth in hymn-like style, giving an inspired message from God. Luke says that he "was filled with the Holy Spirit," and gave words perhaps crafted during many months of silence, now recited with much joy (Luke 1:57–67).

His blessing had two parts. First, he spoke of God's past blessings as He prepared the Way, which we celebrate on Christmas (vv. 68–75); and second, of God's future blessings as the Way is proclaimed (vv. 76–79). This second part, about future blessing, we study today with the help of the Holy Spirit.

God Prepares the Way for Our Future
I. He supplies a messenger; II. He provides a message; III. He prepares a people for a new day.

I. God Supplies a Messenger

The coming of a messenger in John's style was predicted by other prophets. The prophet Elijah made a fiery-chariot exit to God in heaven (2 Kings 2:11–12) and was expected to reappear (Mal. 4:5–6). Many in Jesus' day said Jesus or John were a revived Elijah (Matt. 11:14; Mark 6:14–16; Luke 9:7–9; John 1:21).

Also, a voice had been predicted to cry in the wilderness (Is. 40:3). Such promises came not "by the impulse of man, but men moved by the Holy Spirit spoke from God" (2 Peter 1:21).

God "did not leave Himself without witness" (Acts 14:17). He showed His love and mercy, power and majesty, justice and righteousness. He sent prophets "in many and various ways" (Heb. 1:1). We enter the future with the assurance that God provides messengers (Eph. 4:11–12). He wants all people to call to Him in trouble (Ps. 50:15), and all to be saved (1 Tim. 2:4). But how can they call on God unless they are told, and how they be told unless they are sent (Rom. 10:14–15)?

God personally chose John to prepare His way and point to Christ. God chose Moses and Aaron to teach His laws and sacrifices. God sent Jonah and Daniel among other nations, as He sent innumerable prophets to His own people. Most of them had specific assignments. Our Lord Jesus chose His apostles directly and personally.

In the days since the apostles, God gave His people (His church, His bride, His body) both the authority and the responsibility to select men and women from their midst to positions in the church, to be pastors, teachers, evangelists (Eph. 4:11), bishops (1 Tim. 3:1), elders (Titus 1:5), deacons (1 Tim. 3:8), deaconesses (Rom. 16:1), etc. They are selected and chosen by God's people. They go before the Lord, prepare His ways as His emissaries and ambassadors (2 Cor. 5:20), messengers of His reconciliation and ambassadors preparing the way for the Lord to His people and to others.

In many Christian congregations, such as ours, it is customary to install on the year's first day all elected congregational leaders, who work as servants of the people, with the called and ordained public servant, the pastor, in the work of building His church, training disciples, supplying the congregation with leadership, and assisting all members in their pilgrimage with Christ during the coming year (Eph. 4:11–13).

II. God Prepares the Way for Our Future Not Only with Messengers, but Also with a Message

The message to be proclaimed is one the prophets foretold, although it was at times hidden from them (1 Peter 1:10–11); but now it is fully revealed in Christ. We call that message the Gospel (the Good News), as the angel said: " ... good news of a great joy which will come to all the people" (Luke 2:10). "The Gospel concerning His Son" was "promised beforehand through His prophets in the Holy Scriptures" (Rom. 1:2–3). Zechariah said that John would "go before the Lord to prepare His ways, to give knowledge of salvation to His people in the forgiveness of their sins" (Luke 1:76–77).

And he did that, he gave knowledge: "Behold, the Lamb of God, who takes away the sin of the world!" (John 1:29). He appealed, "Repent!" (Matt. 3:2). When people asked, "What shall we do?" (Luke 3:10–14), his message was not uncertain. Like us they had sins bringing down on them God's judgment. Repentance, forgiveness, new life—all were proclaimed. "The glorious Gospel of the blessed God" (1 Tim. 1:11) was not omitted.

Forgiveness of sins, life, and salvation in Christ's sacrifice was the Gospel Paul said was the power of God unto salvation—a message of which he was not ashamed (Rom. 1:16).

The message of the cross gives courage for our future. It does not mean we have a trick card up our sleeve so that this year we can sin as we please and then quickly rush to use our secret Gospel card to get us out of trouble, free us from guilt. Rather it is that we work and serve God and people, knowing that if we slip or make mistakes, it is not the end of our world. Our heavenly Father loves us.

We hear much today about latchkey children. They can enter the family home anytime they need or desire, but their parents are not home. Praise

God, we too have a key. But more, we have a Father who is there, welcoming us, waiting and caring for us, rushing to our side to forgive and help us in our need.

The past need not worry us, nor the future give us fear, because of God's abiding love in Christ our Savior. He gave us, as Zechariah says, "a horn of salvation" (Luke 1:69), which is always ours for victory over Satan and hell. No ox leaves home without his horns. No unicorn would be caught without his horn. The Christian always has his horn of salvation.

The Holy Bible gives us more knowledge, such as God's laws, statutes, judgments, telling us of His involvement in the history of people, the world, His children. But because of our salvation, proclaimed in the Gospel, we experience what Paul says: "All things are yours, whether Paul or Apollos or Cephas or the world or life or death or the present or the future, all are yours; and you are Christ's; and Christ is God's" (1 Cor. 3:21–23).

III. God Prepares Us to Live in the Shadow of Death for a New Day

Everything our heavenly Father does is good. So speaks Zechariah in His blessing. His messengers "prepare His ways" through His "tender mercy " (Luke 1:76–78). We are reminded of this Old Testament description of God: "The Lord, the Lord, a God merciful and gracious, slow to anger, and abounding in steadfast love and faithfulness, keeping steadfast love for thousands, forgiving iniquity and transgression and sin" (Ex. 34:6–7).

Such mercy is abundant, "new every morning" (Lam. 3:23), and so it has ever been (Ps. 25:6), even before manifested in Christ. It gives light "to those who sit in darkness and in the shadow of death, to guide our feet into the way of peace" (Luke 1:79).

Now and always is the dawn of the continuing day of His shining love, which never ends, not even in eternity. "My God will supply every need of yours according to His riches in glory in Christ Jesus" (Phil. 4:19).

In the darkness we face this year there may be changes for our lives, some we welcome and some we dread. Hours of testings and trials are ahead, but God's right hand is not short nor His mercy withdrawn. Elisha the prophet knew he had his wall of fire to protect him (2 Kings 6:16–17). The devil complained that God put a hedge around His servant Job (Job 1:10). "For I am sure," says Paul, "that neither death, nor life, nor angels, nor principalities, nor things present, *nor things to come,* nor powers, nor height, nor depth, nor anything else in all creation, will be able to separate us from the love of God in Christ Jesus our Lord" (Rom. 8:38–39).

Epiphany

Prepare the Way

For Others

John 1:6–16

Notes

1. A good day for mission festival, featuring foreign missions where God's Word is hidden or darkened. Bible translators or missionaries to fields like the Muslims, the Jews, Russia, China, etc.

2. When Marco Polo in 1295 returned to Venice from China and dictated an account of his experiences, an account which was the chief Renaissance source of information on the East, he relates how they asked him if it were really the way he wrote—"It is more wonderful than anything I have told." People were amazed. Imagine the amazement produced by the Magi returning to the East. What wonderment we can evoke by relating our journey to worship the Christ Child.

3. We generally wrap the gifts we give. We wonder about the content of the mysterious packages under the Christmas tree. Epiphany is the unwrapping and revelation of God's gracious gift, freely bestowed, hitherto a mystery within the plan of God.

4. The text shows that John witnessed or gave testimony to the Light. By giving testimony a person can expose himself to danger, for instance by incriminating himself. To protect themselves, some seek immunity from prosecution. A witness like John testifies to the Light not to darkness, to righteousness not to evil. But even as such a witness he still is exposed to danger and death. Thus Christ, too, for His testimony and revelation was accused of blasphemy. Pray for all those who by life or language witness to Christ.

5. "Grace upon grace" is the closing of the text. The Greek has "charis anti charitos." It is grace in return for grace, grace because of grace. The idea is that it follows without ceasing. It is not exchanging New Testament grace for Old Testament grace, nor being given charismatic grace after saving grace, not one gift and then another. It is rather like a stream constantly flowing. It is a doubling. "To him who has will more be given" (Matt. 13:12).

God holds none of His love back from us. God holds back all of His wrath from us.

6. Herod planned to destroy the Child, similar to the way Haman built a gallows to destroy Mordecai and his people. The Egyptians had a plan to destroy all Israelite baby boys (Ex. 1:16). Saul planned to destroy David through the gift of his daughter (1 Sam. 18:21, 25). There is safety and protection with God. We fear not them who can destroy us but God, "who can destroy both soul and body in hell" (Matt. 10:28).

7. "Epiphany" is used in the New Testament in relation to our Lord's first appearing (2 Tim. 1:10; Titus 2:11; 3:4). All other New Testament references deal with His second or final appearing in glory (2 Thess. 2:8; 1 Tim. 6:14; 2 Tim. 4:8; Titus 2:13)

The Sermon

In Samaria's history (2 Kings 6:24–7:20) Syria once besieged it, resulting in a severe famine. Deeply angry over this, Samaria's king sent an envoy to Elisha, blaming him who had predicted it. Elisha denied the blame, but assured him God would end the famine in 24 hours. Then all would know the power and goodness of the Lord.

One of the king's officers said, "If the Lord Himself should make windows in heaven, could this thing be?"

Elisha answered, "You shall see it with your own eyes, but you shall not eat of it."

That night the well-supplied Syrian enemy heard noises of chariots and supposed that the king of Samaria had hired Hittites and Egyptians to help him. In confusion under darkness they retreated, leaving behind food, battle supplies, and many of their animals.

Four lepers living nearby reasoned that death in the famine-stricken city was certain, whereas the Syrians might give them something to eat. So they entered the Syrian camp but met no one amidst the plentiful food and clothing. While feasting they said, "We are not doing right. This day is a day of good news. . . . Come, let us go and tell the king's household." When it was found that the Syrians really were gone, the people rushed into their camp. When the king's officer who had doubted Elijah's word came there, he was crushed to death by the mob searching for food. Thus Elisha's prophecy was fulfilled.

Spiritually hungry and weak, we came to Bethlehem. God's grace and favor opened the windows of heaven, and He gave us the Savior. We celebrated and trusted in God for the new year. He preserved our lives here and eternally. His grace filled our garner. Our cup of joy ran over with love and forgiveness. His promises crowded our cupboards. He filled our shopping bags with tenderness and kindness.

With the lepers we say, "We are not doing right" to remain silent. "This day is a day of good news.... Come, let us go and tell ... " tell the good news of God's love and forgiveness.

I. Preparing the Way for Others to See God's Work

We dare not hide this, for it is His work. Today is Epiphany, which means manifestation or making known. God made known His gift of the Christ Child. He gave the star to guide the Magi to inquire from His own people where their newborn King was born.

Thirty years later "there was a man sent from God, whose name was John. He came for testimony, to bear witness to the Light, that all might believe." He fulfilled what God had said centuries before, as He prepared a suffering people to receive His love. He spoke through Isaiah (40:1–5): "Comfort, comfort my people, says your God. Speak tenderly to Jerusalem, and cry to her that her warfare is ended, that her iniquity is pardoned.... A voice cries: 'In the wilderness prepare the way of the Lord, make straight in the desert a highway for our God.' Every valley shall be lifted up, and every mountain and hill be made low; the uneven ground shall become level, and the rough places a plain. And the glory of the Lord shall be revealed, and *all flesh shall see it* together, for the mouth of the Lord has spoken." God promises. God reveals. God speaks. It is done.

God Himself named the "man sent from God" as John, which means "Jehovah has been gracious." Already by that name God was preaching His message. That message was not new, although in bad times we wonder where or how He will be gracious. Many could join Job in saying (23:2–6): "My complaint is bitter, [God's] hand is heavy in spite of my groaning. Oh, that I knew where I might find Him, that I might come even to His seat! I would lay my case before Him and fill my mouth with arguments. I would learn what He would answer me.... Would He contend with me in the greatness of His power? No; He would give heed to me."

Our hope for God's love is not new, nor is His reassuring love unusual. Both are old and yet new each day. His love fades not; it is bright through clouds and all seasons. Once God used a star to guide people; generally He uses His Word, which has a reliability record that says, "If we are faithless,

He remains faithful" (2 Tim. 2:13). People can and do rely on Him who loves and cares. "The Lord has been gracious." This caused childless Zechariah and Elizabeth to rejoice. John "came for testimony, to testify to the Light, *that all might believe through him.*" His voice was heard. He directed people to "the Lamb of God, who takes away the sin of the world." This brought results as many repented and believed in the Christ.

John knew that previous prophets had predicted such a voice would speak. He spoke the assigned message, proclaiming it with certainty, in plain words, clearly and distinctly. He told people to repent, to be baptized, to turn to Christ. As a result they, too, saw God's work.

The Word produces results. God has been "found by those who did not seek [Him] (Is. 65:1).

II. God Desires Witness and Testimony

When God called John to *witness,* John was to tell what he saw and heard— the truth, both judgment and promise. A witness cannot tell what he does not know. To do so makes him a false witness. On the other hand, were he not to tell what he knows, he would make himself an unfaithful witness.

The witness about Christ's work dare not be withheld. At the Jerusalem temple our Lord spoke of the world's end thus: "This Gospel of the Kingdom will be preached throughout the whole world, as a testimony to all nations; and then the end will come" (Matt. 24:14). At His ascension Jesus commanded that "repentance and forgiveness of sins should be preached in His name to all nations, beginning from Jerusalem. You are witnesses of these things" (Luke 24:47–48). Before Pentecost He said: "You shall be My witnesses" (Acts 1:8).

It is clear to God's people, whether prophet or apostle, evangelist or ordinary disciple, that all are God's witnesses. One of God's love poems depicts His relation to Israel and asks His beloved to declare His actions, whether of mercy or rebuke. Such telling is anticipated and expected. The poem repeats the word, "You are My witnesses ... and My servant whom I have chosen, that you may know and believe Me.... You are my witnesses.... None can deliver from My hand.... Fear not, nor be afraid; have I not told you from of old and declared it? And you are My witnesses!" (Is. 43:10, 12–13; 44:8).

When we confess the Creed, we testify about Christ and our faith. Paul encourages us to give testimony in life and words. He writes: "Fight the good fight of the faith; take hold of the eternal life to which you were called when you made the good confession in the presence of many witnesses. In the presence of God who gives life to all things, and of Christ Jesus who in His testimony before Pontius Pilate made the good confession . . . " (1 Tim. 6:12–13).

By his testimony to God and His Word, John knew the joy of a witness of the Lord's power and dominion, but he also learned suffering from the dominion and power of those opposed to his witness, and thus he met death and martyrdom. God's witnesses face suffering. That's part of carrying His cross. God may transfer such witnesses from life here to life everlasting, as our hearers change from the death of sin to life in Christ.

Stephen's life showed that. He witnessed for the Lord (Act 7) before the Sanhedrin. They in turn felt that they were witnesses to a "blasphemy" and must help punish and purge out such evil (Deut. 17:2–7). Witnesses of Stephen's witness claimed He blasphemed by confessing Jesus as Messiah. For that they would stone him to death. To do so with vigor, the witnesses placed their outer robes at Saul's feet. Saul witnessed the witness's power and anger.

While Saul was persecuting those who followed the Way, God converted him. He became a faithful witness, not to persecute but to promote the Way. With such missionaries the Lord built a highway for other witnesses around the Roman Empire. By their work many believed, Jew and Gentile. By God's work through such witnesses down through the ages, by the Holy Spirit calling people to faith in Christ, the Way was preserved for others— to this very day and at this church service!

This was the beginning of a new day in God's world for all people. God made a good world, but, prompted by the devil, humans continually make it evil. Now, at the start of the new era, John could say with great immediacy: "The kingdom of heaven is at hand" (Matt. 3:2).

Mark opened his Gospel with the words, "The beginning of the Gospel" and wrote about John (Mark 1). This begins the Good News. This begins the new covenant, the new testament, about which Jeremiah wrote (Jer. 31:31–34). This is the beginning of the Christian church, the communion of saints, of believers. "To all who received Him, who believed in His name, He gave power to become children of God; who were born, not of blood nor of the will of the flesh nor of the will of man, but of God" (John 1:12–13).

Because God cares for others, we "live sober, upright, and godly lives in this world, awaiting our blessed hope, the appearing of the glory of our great God and Savior Jesus Christ" (Titus 2:12–13). Since "the grace of God has appeared for the salvation of all men" (v. 11), we can "always be prepared to make a defense to anyone who calls [us] to account for the hope that is in [us]" (1 Peter 3:15) and so manifest and reveal His love.

Notes

Notes

Notes

Notes